"Using her experiences from Australia to Texas and all over the world, Ryan explores her own personal journey as a gift to all of us. At times poignant, at times triumphant, her story is always inspiring."

BETTY SUE FLOWERS, former director Lyndon Baines Johnson Library and Museum, Emeritus Professor of English at University of Texas at Austin, poet, author, editor, and television host

"Pam Ryan is an exceptional and remarkable person with a combination of intelligence and empathy. She is a force for good in the advancement of humankind in a challenging world. As founder of Psychology Beyond Borders, aimed at reducing psychological suffering in many affected populations around the world, Pam demonstrates her deep understanding of the steps needed to ease trauma in people's lives."

BOB HAWKE, former Prime Minister of Australia

"The words 'I don't know who I am until I see what I do' will stay with me forever. Learning to embrace the light and the dark, to touch the smooth and the rough, to fully appreciate one you must know the other—Pamela Ryan's important knowledge and wisdoms are told with such simple beauty. Life can be a carpet —we can be the magic!"

GILL HICKS, MBE, author, founder of M.A.D. for Peace, and survivor of terrorist bombings, London, July 2005

"This book shows us not only how to negotiate the inevitable bumps and troughs in life but also how to reach for the peaks. It reflects Pamela Ryan's experience of repeatedly turning improbable aspirations and unpromising circumstances into impressive achievements."

SIR ROGER JOWELL, social scientist and professor, London School of Economics, London

"After reading *Magic Carpet Flying* I am physically, emotionally and mentally awake. What Pamela Ryan is sharing with readers is so profound. While reading these pages, I thought of the darkest moments in my life, the losses I have experienced, and the struggle I am going through in my efforts to build democracy in Cambodia.

"Flying a 'magic carpet' is a lonely flight if not shared with others, as the deep ends that the magic carpet takes us to are the unknown holes of our lives we are not willing or are afraid to explore. Dr. Pamela Ryan takes us with her to those deep ends, and her willingness to invite us to fly the magic carpet with her is a journey of light even in the darkest moments of despair and loss."

MU SOCHUA, social worker, Member of Parliament, Cambodia

"Pam Ryan has already had a brilliant career—flying through all kinds of exotic, exhausting, and exhilarating skies. Wherever she lands she makes a difference. She also brings hope and inspires people to do things they sometimes never thought they could! Pam is one of those inspirational, can-do characters who'll always make room on her magic carpet for anyone who's prepared to make the journey. I know. I've flown with her more than once."

RAY MARTIN, international television journalist, including *60 Minutes,* Australia

"Pamela Ryan has written an extraordinary memoir. Her ability to reflect upon and articulate her triumphs and tragedies with clarity of thought and magical prose is exceptionally profound—an inspiration for all ages."

MARY MARGARET FARABEE, founding chair, Texas Book Festival

MAGIC CARPET FLYING

MAGIC CARPET FLYING
THE RIDE OF YOUR LIFE

PAMELA RYAN

Blue Butterfly Books
THINK FREE, BE FREE

Blue Butterfly Book Publishing Inc.
2583 Lakeshore Boulevard West
Toronto, Ontario, Canada M8V 1G3
Tel 416-255-3930   Fax 416-252-8291
Ordering information: www.bluebutterflybooks.ca

First edition, soft cover: 2009

Library and Archives Canada Cataloguing in Publication

Ryan, Pamela, 1957–
Magic carpet flying : the ride of your life / Pamela Ryan.

ISBN 978-0-9784982-5-2

1. Self-actualization (Psychology). I. Title.

BF637.S4R925 2009   158.1   C2009-900526-3

Design and typesetting by Fox Meadow Creations
Text set in Adobe Garamond

Blue Butterfly Books thanks book buyers
for their support in the marketplace.

Contents

Introduction

Some of us meander through our lives, going with the flow, bending with the twists and turns, plowing through, jumping over, sliding under or simply avoiding the obstacles in our path, with no urge to question, no urge to dissect retrospectively or prospectively how or why we experience what we do. In contrast, others of us spend endless hours introspecting about our life's journey, constantly rehashing the past and re-envisioning the future, seeking answers to the age old questions of "Why am I here?" "What can I learn from this?" and "Where do I go from here?"

Like most of us, I fall somewhere in between these two extremes. So when I was invited to deliver the Commencement (Graduation) Address at the University of South Australia, the invitation triggered for me a unique opportunity to take the precious time to introspect—to ask those questions: What have I learned? What are the essential messages from my life so far? How might the lessons that have forced themselves upon me be useful to others facing similar life situations?

MAGIC CARPET FLYING

This opportunity to reflect on my own journey—one that has taken me from a colorful, but simple childhood in an outback Australian mining town to a complex, virtually global citizen's existence—was a gift.

I was shocked when I calculated just how long ago I stood in my own cap and gown excitedly receiving my Bachelor of Arts degree as an idealistic twenty-one-year-old. Time has flown! And *flying*, or more specifically, *magic carpet flying*, is the theme for the reflections I want to share.

A friend recently retired after thirty years as a television journalist. He smilingly described his thirty years with the television network as "a magic carpet ride." His whimsical description really resonated with me. My journey since first graduating has also been a magic carpet ride. And I am hoping that when you look back on your life, that you look back in wonder at *your* magic carpet ride.

WHAT DO WE KNOW ABOUT CARPET RIDES?

Carpet rides of all kinds share some basic characteristics:

➤ Carpet rides go up and they go down. The journey *always* includes both ascent and descent;

➤ Your carpet ride will include periods of

straight and level flight when you are in equilibrium, just cruising, on automatic pilot;

➤ Carpets fly at varying altitudes and speeds depending upon what is happening in the environment in which we fly, as well as inside our own bodies. You will experience a number of different altitudes and speeds throughout your journey;

➤ Sometimes you will fly solo; other times you will fly with a group;

➤ Sometimes your journey will be at the mercy of others; sometimes other people will be at your mercy, their carpet rides dependent upon you;

➤ Extraordinary flight maneuvers require extraordinary preparation and training. Sometimes you will be the learner, sometimes, the instructor;

➤ Every carpet ride involves turbulence—at times expected, at other times not. You may experience periods where you feel jolted by disequilibrium. Some carpet rides encounter turbulence so severe—buffeting storms, complete with lightening strikes, thunder, and destabilizing wind shear—that you may wonder if you will get through. For a few of us, the storms may be so bad that we crash, or at least have to attempt an emergency landing, perhaps nowhere near our intended destination;

➤ Sometimes you will be flying in the dark. You will feel lost, disoriented;

➤ And sometimes you will soar through the light—dancing with the wind, laughing with the sun, basking in wonder and joy at all that you see, know and feel.

I have been both witness and bearer of the extremes of carpet flying.

In my work

In Ethiopia, I have looked into the sad and shamed faces of women emaciated by malnutrition, pregnancy and childbirth before their bodies were ready. These women had spent days in labor, unable to get the medical help they needed, their babies stillborn, their internal organs sometimes ripped apart;

In Sri Lanka, I have walked the decimated beaches with students and teachers who outran a thirty-foot-high wave and bravely returned to the beach hours later to bury the dead;

In East Timor, I have witnessed the determination of women trying to forge a better future for their kids, themselves and their country, often after years of sexual abuse;

In South Africa, I have sung and danced with the children whose families were wiped out by HIV/AIDS. Some of these kids had been savagely raped because of the virgin-cure myth and the complete breakdown of social structures and mores in the wake of loss, despair and hopelessness;

In the USA, on the fifth anniversary of the

September 11 terror attacks, I have descended into the pit of Ground Zero and felt the palpable, searing pain of collective loss. In the aftermath of Hurricane Katrina in 2006, on the curbs of New Orleans streets, I sat and cried with single mums and their kids, amid thirty-foot-high piles of rubble, as they wondered how they could possibly start over;

In outback Australia, I have felt the pain of the Aboriginal men who shared their stories of being removed from the only homes they knew, to be forever torn between two cultures;

Next week, I fly to Uganda to meet with war-affected kids, many of whom were child soldiers who have witnessed and/or perpetrated some of the most horrific acts of violence that human beings can inflict on each other.

In my personal life

I have seen the devastating toll that mental illness, other disease and early death extracts from those who suffer, and all who love them. My dad was diagnosed with paranoid schizophrenia when I was about seven. He died when I was fifteen. Like others diagnosed with paranoid schizophrenia, my dad heard persuasive voices in his head. He truly believed those voices represented forces trying to destroy him (and his family). Like Nobel Laureate John Nash, my dad suffered through electroshock treatment and debilitating, mind-numbing drugs. In those days, these were the only treatments the health care professions could offer. Unlike John Nash, my dad was not able to manage his illness. By the last year of his life, the voices my dad heard were so powerful he could no longer bear them. Like others diagnosed with mental illness, he was severely depressed. To kill the voices, he had to kill himself. He could see no other alternative. He fatally shot himself five months after his forty-eighth birthday.

Not long after our dad died, my sister was

diagnosed with the recurrence of a life-threatening blood disease (which had almost killed her when she was two years old) and had her spleen removed. A couple of years after she recovered, my brother was diagnosed with kidney malfunction, a lifelong condition that continues to challenge, but not define him. About six years after my brother's initial diagnosis, my mum died of a rare form of cancer.

By the time I graduated with a Bachelors degree, death, dying and chronic life-threatening illness were familiar passengers on our family carpet ride.

Light

But while my carpet ride catapulted me through darkness, both at work and at home, I have always been surrounded by light. While I have been confronted by the depths of sadness and the worst horrors human beings can inflict on each other (or on themselves), what stands out most for me is survival, healing, hope, happiness ... life.

In both my life and my work, I see evidence that most of us not only ultimately cope after heart-wrenching tragedy, we can grow.

From my work with Psychology Beyond Borders in communities around the world that have faced incomprehensible adversity, I have learned that while we may never get over horror, we can get through it. And getting through horror is often made possible by the caring presence of others who help illuminate the way forward.

The enduring images I have from Ethiopia, Sri Lanka, East Timor, South Africa, the USA, Australia, and my own childhood in Broken Hill, are:

Images of profound strength;

Of intimate human connection;

Of people doing good for each other;

People being there for each other;

People being there for me.

I picture joyous, expectant smiling eyes: faces lighting up with glee at the sight of their own images on camera, and little black hands reaching out for mine as we walked in the dust.

I picture Muslim women in their hijabs singing "Waltzing Matilda"—side by side with "ocker" Aussie men, celebrating our common humanity.

I picture the looks on mothers' faces as they make candles or jewelry, earning a living to build a future where they had thought they had none.

I picture what happens when people from starkly different backgrounds get to know those whom they fear.

I picture the vibrant, toothless, life-filled grin of an old woman who had lost every family member (including her eight children and their children) in a war she had not condoned being lovingly embraced by an entire village as everyone's "Grannie," testament to the potent healing power of social support and human connection.

I picture people all over the world rising out of the most desperate of circumstances, and choosing life, even when they had witnessed so much pain, or death...

And I picture some of the most passionate, dedicated altruistic professionals on the planet—people who are committed to helping those in their journey through horror.

In my personal life, while I can recall the despair of my own family each time the universe plummeted us into the worst possible storms, what I remember most is the strength, the resilience, the immeasurable courage of my mother, my sister, my brother and my father.

I see a childhood filled with love and laughter because our mother chose to embrace the light, not the dark.

I visualize the incredible support of friends

and extended family—amazing beautiful gifts, each and every one of them: people who celebrate with me when I am glowing with joy, and who commiserate with me when I feel pummelled by sorrow or anguish.

By experiencing both the ups and downs of carpet flying, I know that when we face some of the worst things that can happen to us, we can also learn the best, that:

We can be strong;

Others love and value us;

We love and value others; and

We can have a lasting positive impact on the lives and beings of others, as they can on us.

So my carpet ride has left indelibly imprinted images, not of darkness, but of light, and not of horror, but of hope. And it is seeing the light, the hope and the life in the darkness that has been one of the biggest sources of magic for me.

HOW CAN YOU CREATE YOUR OWN
MAGICAL CARPET RIDE?

1. Know what is magical for you

Magic for one person can be a nightmare for others. You may not know what is magical until you do something and reflect back on what you did. The professor who most influenced me during my studies toward my Ph.D. at the University of Texas, Karl Weick, had a mantra: "I don't know what I think until I see what I say." I have extended his mantra: "I don't know who I am until I see what I do." The very acts of saying and doing give us the raw materials for defining what we think and who we are, for illuminating our own magic.

So to find your own magic, look back on what you have been doing. If what you have been doing ignites your passion, is replenishing of your spirit, is life-giving, then it is magic. If what you have been doing is life-depleting, if it does not feel right... it is not magic. And if what you are doing is not magic, then know you can walk away, even if your escape is via the infinite pathways of your mind. Go try some more activities until your passion is ignited!

Living my truth

I have learned that magic for me is about "living my Truth," both to myself and to others. Living "Truth" begins with voicing truth. Sometimes it is hardest to voice truth to myself, because confronting truth may mean acknowledging something I do not want to know, that others do not want to know. But I have come to accept that even the most difficult of truths must be voiced, because once voiced, the way is cleared for us to "do." For me, living my truth means not just speaking out against injustice, but doing something, however small. Living my truth also means speaking out honestly, openly and caringly about the tough issues, including suicide and mental illness.

And I have found that magic multiplies when you live truth, when you live your passion. You tend to be excited, enthusiastic, happy. And it's contagious. You exude light, and because you exude light you attract light. And because you attract light, people treat you as though you are light. This creates a type of self-fulfilling prophecy, where the passion and strength of your beliefs about what you are doing infuses in others the same belief in your capacity to realize your passions. And they treat you in ways that convey and reinforce those beliefs. Along this path, you meet others in the same headspace (as well as airspace) who share your passion. And before you know it, the energy you radiate joins with the energy of others on the same flight-path, in the same light. The resulting synergy is potent. It's called *synchronicity*. You will be incredulous at who and what you encounter! And you will be incredulous at what you can achieve.

2. Select a magical destination and go for it

Point your carpet in the direction of the magic and enjoy the journey. I learned the hard way that it is easy to get so fixated on the destination, that we don't notice the flying.

When I first left university with my Bachelor's degree in the 1980s, I had a clearly defined career plan. I knew what I was going to achieve by when. But then I fell in love with an American: my carefully delineated career path imploded, and I found myself in the USA. My envisaged brilliant career was not so brilliant in an alien environment. But then I started my Ph.D. at the University of Texas, and I studied organizations that succeeded by being opportunistic, by being adept at going with the flow of their environments, by being adaptable. I learned flexibility could not only be good, but in "going with the flow," in making myself up as I went along (while not losing sight of the star or planet to which I ultimately wanted to fly), I could create new flight paths, discover new galaxies and land in places I might never have envisaged when setting out.

So instead of adhering to a rigid step-by-step plan, I discovered I could actually achieve more by having a flight path with very broad leeway. I could move toward my destination without having to follow a narrowly defined route. The key is to both plan, and not plan, to have a map, and no map. A wonderful case study, summarized by Karl Weick in his book, *Sense-making in Organizations* (first related by Hungarian Nobel Laureate Albert Szent-Gyorti, later preserved in a poem by Holub in 1977), illustrates this:

During World War II, a Hungarian army regiment was engaged in military training exercises in Switzerland. The young commanding officer sent a troop of soldiers into the mountains on an "outward bound" style of mission. Not long after they were dispatched, a severe snowstorm hit and the troop became lost. When the troop was two days late returning, the commanding officer became gravely concerned, fearing he had sent his soldiers to their death. When the beleaguered troop finally arrived into base camp on the third day, the relieved commanding officer asked how the men had found their way back without a map. They revealed that, indeed, one troop member did have a map, a fact that enabled them to calm down, plan their action and find their way back to base camp. When the commanding officer scrutinized the map, however, he discovered it was a map of the Pyrenees Mountains. These men were in the Swiss Alps.

A true story! What this anecdote reveals is that maps animate and orient us. With a map, this World War II regiment was able to remain active and develop a defined purpose; they were able to create an image of where they were and an image of where they were headed, so they kept on moving, kept noticing cues, kept updating their sense of where they were... and found their way to their ultimate destination.

When you allow yourself a flight path with a broad ambit and a loosely defined path in the general direction of your destination, you can be playful. And being playful can bring unexpected joy as you discover people, places and spaces you may not have known existed.

It may not surprise you to know that I have been learning to fly a plane. As part of my cross-country flight training last year, I asked my instructor if I could fly to Broken Hill, my home town in the middle of the Australian outback. When he and I were planning our route, he said: "Do you want to fly straight there or do you want to muck around a bit and zigzag on the way?" Of course I chose to "muck around and zigzag." As a result, I discovered all sorts of wonders along the way, elements of the outback route I had driven and flown so many times, but had never seen. By allowing myself to zigzag, I experienced the exhilaration of both the journey and of our landing at the Broken Hill airport!

So I encourage you, as part of making yourself up as you go along (within the broad parameters of the flight path toward your ultimate destination), to experiment with zigzagging by using any map that broadly reflects the territory in which you want to fly. Any map will ensure that you fly in the general direction of your defined magic, because it will set you in motion and keep you cognizant of where you are, versus where you want to go. You may be surprised at what and whom you experience along the way.

3. Be the Pilot-in-Command

It sounds basic, but so many of us live other people's lives—the flight paths set in motion by the lives our parents wanted for us, the lives our partners live, the life and experiences that have defined us until now. Being the Pilot-in-Command means being the one who designs and enacts your own carpet ride. It means forging your own flight path, not flying in the wake of others; it means changing your flight path if the one you've set does not feel right to you. Being the Pilot-in-Command means living your truth, your core values, living what ignites your passion.

Sometimes a single flight (or story) may start to dominate our identity, who we present to others, how others see us. But every human being is more complicated than just one flight, one dimension. Our challenge is to think about all the other aspects of who we are that also reflect who we want to be. At any given point in our lives, we have the power to re-define our flight path, how we fly, what we fly, who we are. So I encourage you to continually define your own flight path by looking back at where you have flown, and ahead to where you want to be—and maintain or change your heading accordingly.

4. Prepare and train for your ride

Being Pilot-in-Command and making yourself up as you go along is nowhere near as easy, or chaotic, as it sounds. To be ready, willing and able to soar beyond average destinations, to fly loop de loops, to negotiate inevitable storms, or even finesse a crash landing, we need to be skilled to fly well. No good pilot will attempt a maneuver (climbing, stalling, spins) for which they, or their plane, are not equipped. There are many things we can do to help ourselves be as ready as we can be for whatever or whomever we encounter as we fly.

Connecting with others makes extraordinary flying possible and fun

I have been able to enact some of the hardest maneuvers of my life because of the people who fly with me. So much of what I have done is with other people—at Issues Deliberation Australia, Psychology Beyond Borders, the Silverton Foundation, the University of South Australia—flying with colleagues, friends and family who share similar truths, similar destinations. I could never have achieved what I have achieved without these amazing people flying by my side. And in flying together, we have discovered how much we can do, both as individuals or as a group.

Learning is forever

Continuing to learn and discover new things are also magical for me.

Education is a beautiful thing. Those of us who complete a formal tertiary education are fortunate. For me, completing high school and university studies was a huge step in helping me to prepare myself for magic carpet flying. But over ten per cent of the world's peoples do not even get a primary school education. Eight hundred million adults cannot read or write. Today, eighty million kids don't even go to school—and women and girls lose out the most. I was one of the lucky ones. But education is a universal right of all human beings.

Education can be a life-long process. And neuropsychologists tell us this is a good thing. By continuing to fire neurons down new pathways in our brains, we not only ward off Alzheimer's, but we continually open ourselves to new experiences and new opportunities for magic.

And I have learned that for the most daunting of activities perseverance and tenacity are key.

The importance of perseverance and tenacity became particularly poignant for me when I started learning to fly a plane at the age of fifty. One of the most challenging aspects of learning to fly was mastering talking on the radio to the air traffic control tower. I am not unused to publicly speaking to hundreds of people or conducting media interviews on live television and radio, but sit me behind the microphone in a little Cessna talking live to air traffic control with who knows who listening...

During my first few flights, when air traffic controllers needed me to respond back to their fast-paced instructions (delivered in a clipped Texan twang), I would look at my instructor in complete panic and say "You do it!" But I was determined ... so for hours and hours and hours I listened on my computer to live air traffic control conversations (wearing my pilot's headset), responding out loud as if I was in the plane. It took me months to get comfortable. When I finally made my first smooth, seemingly unflustered call, the clearly amused air traffic controller came back with: "Excellent radio call Cessna 52208, but you are on the wrong frequency. But call us any time to practice!"

Education is not just about being equipped to react to what is happening in our airspace, being prepared to enter uncharted airspace, or ensuring you have the necessary skills to tackle new flight paths or new maneuvers. It is also about being prepared to *detect* opportunities when they occur. A good pilot is constantly scanning the environment, inside the plane (including their own bodies), as well as in a 360-degree circle outside the plane.

Those successful, flexible companies I studied as an organizational psychologist were not only prepared to act effectively when opportunity knocked, but could *see* opportunity in the first place. And the "Law of Requisite Variety" tells us that only complex organisms can detect complexity in their environment. When we complicate ourselves, we expand the number of neural networks firing in our brains. (It is like creating whole new neighborhoods, even suburbs, in the "street map" of your brain!) The more complex we are, the more "neural neighborhoods" we activate, the more opportunities we will see and the more opportunities we will be able to act upon.

So one of the strategies for creating more opportunity for magic is to increase your own complexity—think, do, "be," outside your own box as often as you can stand it. You might be surprised at how this simple strategy increases your creativity and helps you think and venture beyond your own boundaries.

Mind, Body, Spirit

Successful flying requires integration between the Mind, the Body and the Spirit. No astute pilot will attempt to fly if their mind, their body or their spirit is ailing. The consequences are too grave. This has probably been the single biggest lesson I have learned in the last few years.

My area of speciality as a research psychologist has been cognition—how people think, how they process information, how they represent what they experience in their brains. And as you might expect from this specialty, while athletic, I have always been someone who lives in her head.

I have learned the hard way to listen to the information my body is giving me.

The universe has delivered many lessons... When my mum first heard that my dad had shot himself, she and my sister and I were in

Adelaide on vacation. The three of us had to fly back to Broken Hill immediately, leaving our car behind. It was my first time in a plane. I sat in the bulkhead seat and cried and vomited all the way home. I had not been told what had happened, just that there was some kind of emergency. But despite not being told anything, I sensed, by the actions and reactions of my family members who did know, that something dire had occurred. When the flight attendant asked my mother what was wrong with me, my mother told her that we had had to fly home suddenly, that this was my first time on a plane—and perhaps this was so distressing me. My body knew differently. My body sensed and responded to what my thinking brain could neither comprehend nor translate into words.

It took me about five years to be able to fly in any plane—sitting anywhere, let alone sit in a bulkhead seat—without vomiting. It took perseverance, lots of calming breathing exercises and positive self-talk to overcome the powerful message my body continued to give me, long after the emergency had passed. Flying in a plane in the bulkhead seat clearly evoked a myriad of painful associations that I ultimately learned to manage. These days, not only do I get in and out of planes without any anxiety, I am exhilarated by flying the plane myself, and do so at every opportunity.

And my work over the past few years affirms that such bodily reactions are normal responses to abnormal events. Research on the impacts of psychological trauma repeatedly reveals (as Eastern cultures have known for millennia) that the human body bears the record of the psychological pain and joy our brains register. Sometimes, these earlier experiences may themselves be forgotten by our conscious thinking brains. Our bodies are "hard-wired" through millions of years of evolutionary adaptation to respond to stimuli in specific ways. Research tells us that when an emotion (either positive or negative) is triggered, it can spark a whole sequence of mind-body activities—sometimes without our will or knowledge. For example, in response to sensed danger, just one image, whether imagined or witnessed, can cause our brains to spark the release of chemicals into our bodies, sending messages to our muscles to ready us for fight, flight or freezing (momentary paralysis). We experience changes in our heartbeat, our breathing, our perspiration, the rate at which our blood pumps toward our limbs. All of these bodily responses ready us for fighting the perceived threat, running from it, or being stuck, frozen in place—all pre-programmed coping mechanisms of the human species. Sometimes, the original vivid experience is so powerful that our bodies often retain the set of electrochemical responses the original jolting experience set in motion—a whole kaleidoscope of emotions that later unrelated events can trigger.

Growing up in the outback of Australia, where we were lucky to see nine inches of rainfall a year, opportunities to swim were not exactly abundant, and so I was not a very competent swimmer as a child. I had two near-drowning experiences when I was around eight or nine years old. In one incident, I sank to the bottom of the deep end of a friend's swimming pool. My dad literally fished me out by my pony-tail. In the second incident, I was in the ocean at one of South Australia's stunningly beautiful surfing beaches. As I was swept under by an unexpected wave, I felt myself being sucked down to the bottom of the ocean floor, embroiled in a vortex of sand and surf, swallowing huge amounts of salt water. Although traumatic at the time, as I grew, that experience faded into the deep recesses of my brain and I forgot about it.

Fast-forward twenty years. As an adult, I was determined to master swimming—its benefits for exercise (and safety!) were too compelling. By the time I turned forty, I was ready to tackle my first triathlon. Having trained religiously for months in all three components (swimming, cycling, running), I felt confident, particularly about the swimming, a strong focus of my preparations. I believed I was primed for the 750-meter open-water swim, the first leg of the "tri." The morning of the race, I woke with an enormous knot in my stomach, and vomited several times. This response baffled the thinking me. By the day of the race, I was comfortably swimming several miles a week. But the moment I dove into that lake, with several hundred others, I was flooded, both physically and metaphorically, with flashback images of the two near-drowning incidents from my childhood. I know now that flashbacks are a typical response to traumatizing events. My body had stored those memories that were now threatening to overwhelm me, even though my conscious thinking brain had not recalled these incidents until I was in the water. Mastering those unconscious and automatic physical responses became an imperative, both on that day and afterward. In time and with perseverance, as with flying, I learned to listen to my body, and manage the responses it sometimes enacted without my control.

By my second triathlon (eight years later!), I no longer experienced the flashbacks, so the swim was much easier. Although it was not without its traumatic moments! But with more training, and more open water swims, I was able to conquer that automatic bodily response. Recently, while in the Caribbean, I experienced a bad fall on the boat we were sailing. I fell backwards headfirst down the stairs. Several days later, I immersed my battered body into the cold ocean and swam the half mile or so to shore, knowing the movement through the icy salt water would be healing, both for my body and my spirit. About half way through the swim, I looked back at the boat and ahead to the shore, realizing I was out in the middle of a deep, deep ocean swimming...This time, my brain released chemicals of delight into my body, thrilled that I was able to swim at all! I continue to swim anywhere that I can, as often as I can, and when I do, the sequence of electro-chemical reactions sent relaying through my body represent positive emotions—of delight, of triumph, of peace. Not panic or fear.

So, I have learned, despite being someone with a well-honed determination to think her way through everything, that heeding the lessons of my body will be a lifelong lesson! I now know that if I am not listening, my body tends to do something dramatic to make me listen!

I know also, that it takes both the brain *and* the body to soar with the spirit. For truly magical flying, the Mind, Body and Spirit are inseparable. So I encourage you to constantly explore ways to grow and nurture your mind, body and spirit.

5. Don't forget your own insignificance —have fun

Despite the pain I have witnessed, or perhaps because of it, I find intense joy in what I do and the people with whom I do it. I feel truly blessed to be able to choose life, to choose magic every day that I am alive. Life is too short not to have fun.

And in case I start to get carried away with my own importance, my body and mind seem to conspire to ensure I laugh at myself.

A few months ago, I was meeting with the United Nation's Under-Secretary General for Humanitarian Affairs in New York, a meeting the Psychology Beyond Borders team had been trying to facilitate for some time. On the morning of my meeting, as always, I was trying to multi-task, finish just one more email, swim one more lap ... whatever I could squeeze into my day. After my swim, I frantically threw on my dress—a very long, very fitted dress with a fabulous vibrant African design on fabric made of mesh—with the accompanying long slip. I ran to the elevator to head down the thirty-five floors or so to the hotel lobby. I noticed in the mirror in the elevator that the dress and the slip were a bit out of synch with each other. I needed to straighten the dress out by pulling the slip down. So I bent over to do so, only to discover that the more I pulled, the more slip filled my hands. Apparently, I had not pulled my arms through the straps of the slip when I hurriedly stepped into the dress! So, picture a six-foot-tall blonde, bent over double, hair cascading to her ankles, frenetically pulling her slip from beneath a long mesh dress, glancing up every few seconds to monitor the free fall of the elevator, only to find that the doors opened as the full slip fell around her feet. All I could do was step out of the slip, straighten up to my full height and confidently walk out into the lobby of this very swanky hotel, past all the businessmen and diplomats, in my see-through dress, as if I had my most professional business suit on. I slunk into the hotel spa, calmly explaining: "Fashion emergency, where can I change?" For the rest of the day, when in meetings with various dignitaries at the UN, when I caught a glimpse of that dress in any reflecting surface, I could only laugh, unable to get too carried away with being the girl from Broken Hill in the big city!

So no matter what we are doing and no matter where we are, it is so, so important to laugh often, to find fun, light, hope and life.

In his final hours, my dad could not see the light, the hope or the life. He could not see beyond a single solution. He did not know how to think outside of his box of limited alternatives. He did not know how to manage the panic engulfing his brain or his body. But the rest of my family, despite being deluged by darkness, could and do see the light.

And I see the light, the hope and the life in my own two precious daughters. My heart sings when I see how they embrace life with playfulness, honesty, integrity, compassion. They daily teach me more about living truth than they will ever know.

As a child growing up with the unique Australian outback desert sky, I would look up at night in total awe of the Milky Way stretching out into black infinity. I would imagine myself flying among the stars, gleefully sliding down the slope of a crescent moon. These days I look up with a knowing smile: I have been blessed to fly among the stars of the Milky Way, beyond the Milky Way. My magic carpet ride has taken me to far-flung solar systems and undiscovered universes—galaxy-hopping journeys of my mind, body and spirit with the most life-enriching traveling companions; a carpet ride I could never have dreamed about as I stood with my fellow young graduates thirty years ago, not even in my wildest imaginings.

My favorite poet, T.S. Eliot, said in *East Coker* in *The Four Quartets*: "...the darkness shall be the light, and the stillness the dancing."

As the ride of your life propels you into your next chapter, I encourage you to point your carpet toward the stars. As you fly on, my wishes for you are that you:

➤ Embrace both the light and the darkness, both the stillness and the dancing, all of which will be your journey—and grow from the knowledge inherent in each;

➤ Experience the peace and contentment of living your truth;

➤ Feel the enlightenment that can come from balance between your mind, body and spirit;

➤ Discover the thrill of zigzagging within a very broad ambit toward your envisaged destination;

➤ Welcome the challenge of venturing beyond your own airspace;

➤ Experience the rewards of finding solutions outside your box, even outside all known boxes;

➤ Revel in the sustaining force of those who love and care for you, and in the sustaining force of your love and care for them;

➤ Rejoice in the presence of the fellow travellers who surprise you, extend you and enrich you;

➤ Know the joy of giving of yourself to others in less fortunate circumstances;

➤ Look back from middle (or old!) age in awe and wonder at the light and the magic that was encoded in your body, your mind and your spirit through all your years of flight.

I believe we all can and will use the blessed gift of education—in its myriad forms—to make a difference to our world.

Happy Flying…

FORTHWARD

A note on the "Forthward"

Another of my favorite poets, Mattie Stepanek, who died just weeks before his fourteenth birthday, wanted the final chapter of the last book he published (with former president Jimmy Carter), *Just Peace: A Message of Hope*, to be a "Forthward." He told Carter: "A foreword was when you write something before a book text. A 'Forthward' is where do we go from here? After you read my book, after you read my poems, after you consider all the exchanges of information concerning me and Jimmy Carter and other famous people, then where do we go?"

And so, when I was invited to publish this graduation address as a book, I felt that so much had happened in the few weeks following the address that a "Forthward" was integral to those earlier reflections on light in the darkness, integral to how any of us move forward embracing both light and dark.

FORTHWARD

**How does one find light
in the darkness?**

When I wrote *Magic Carpet Flying*, I did so
looking back over the carpet ride I had lived so
far—reflecting on the ascents and descents, the
peaks and the valleys of the land and skyscape
that constituted my life. I believed, then, that I
had witnessed and experienced the extremes of
light and darkness. But just days after publicly
sharing *Magic Carpet Flying* in an address to

graduating students at an Australian university, I was thrown into an opaque black vortex, so powerful it felt as though it would surely knock the Milky Way from its axis, ensuring I could never again venture beyond those luminous borders.

For me, darkness has typically visited in the form of death—death of a loved one, death of a relationship, death of a trust, death of an envisaged future. These deaths have irrevocably carved cavernous valleys into the geography of my being. With time and distance, I have come to value those valleys—without them, I would not be who I am. But just as some peaks—the very brightest, most joyous summits of our lives—tower above the others, so too do some valleys plunge deeper than the rest. I did not know, as I stood before the graduates and their families sharing the peaks and valleys of my magic carpet ride, the most challenging valley was yet to come.

He and I both sensed that our connection was extraordinary, "extra-earthly." We were not married. We were not partners in a public, traditional sense. We were not partners in a daily living sense. We were partners in an eternal, cosmic sense. Our connection was so outside "normal" life, that we told virtually no one. Kierkegaard said, in the preface to *Either/Or:* "Maybe you've kept a secret in your heart that you felt in all its joy and pain was too precious to share with someone else?" He and I felt that the universe had bestowed upon us a once-in-millions-of-lifetimes precious gift—the two of us connecting so profoundly that our connection could not be captured within the boundedness of mere words. And we knew the nature and profundity of our connection could hardly be conveyed to anyone else. As he said, our experience together defies the adequacy of language. In defying the adequacy of language, our connection did not fit into any previously known script. It did not fit into even the most wildly imagined script. It did not fit into any future script. Instead, this extraordinary human connection registered in a different realm, far from the minutiae of daily life, yet forever present, engraved in the minds, bodies and souls of the two people who experienced it—encoded in the very essence of their beings, imprinted in every cell ... reflected in every star that witnessed their carpet soaring together beyond the Milky Way.

We also knew this was a connection so profound it existed outside of earthly conceptions of time, place or space. As in Kahlil Gibran's *The Prophet*, we were "born together and together forevermore.... Till the white wings of death scatter [our] days.... Together In the silent memory of God." We had found each other at T.S. Eliot's still point (*Four Quartets*)—where the intricate dance of past and future erupted in each Kundalini Rising present. We were the clay so liltingly depicted by Irish poet and philosopher John O'Donahue in *Anam Cara*:

> ...*It is as if millions of years before, your lover's clay and your clay lay side by side. Then in the turning of the seasons, your one clay divided and separated. You begin to rise as distinct clay forms, each housing a different individuality and destiny.... your clay selves wandered for thousands of years through the universe [and when you meet]...there is an awakening between you, an ancient knowing, Love opens the door of ancient recognition. You enter. You come home to each other....*

He and I came home to each other as unique equals—in mind, body and spirit—two parts of the one clay finding its missing piece...amid millennia of separate wanderings. When asked how long we were "together," I would say,

"From the end of time to the beginning of time," perhaps instinctively tapping into the ancient knowing of our primordial connection. As American poet Maya Angelou so poignantly described: "When the first stone looked up at the blazing sun and the first tree struggled up from the forest floor .... We loved each other in and out, in and out, in and out of time."

We eerily shared passions and aspects of our histories and lives too numerous to count—both avid thinkers, writers, teachers, swimmers, cyclists, pilots, travellers ... simultaneously engaging in so many of the same activities no matter what our individual contexts. Some twenty years before we read each other's writings, we had both theorized on similar topics, using virtually the same words. Whole paragraphs could have been substituted into each other's pages. And we were writing on continents 12,000 miles apart, writing for different arenas, writing with no knowledge of the other's work.

With both of us explorers of the human brain and behavior—prone to seek explanations of the inexplicable, to try to make sense of the nonsensical—the latest science contained some clues about the extraordinariness of our experience together. We mused that maybe the two of us had more mirror neurons firing simultaneously with each other than with any other human on the planet...

Mirror neurons are a relatively recent discovery, the product of a burgeoning area of brain research in which high resonance imaging is employed to map brain activity. I have been excitedly following these developments in neuroscience ever since they first emerged in the late 1990s. What this research tells us is that when the brains of two interacting people are mapped while executing and observing actions of intent, the same areas of the brain light up simultaneously in each person. These brain cells, and the neural networks they constitute when clumped together as groups, fire up equally in both people (in a mirror-like way, in real time) when one person performs an action and when one *witnesses* the other performing the action. In such pairings, even though we might be just witnessing another's action, our brains act as if we ourselves had enacted the activity, our brain cells triggering exactly the same sequence of bodily reactions, the same emotions. The very same areas of the brain, virtually identical neural pathways, are activated in both people at the very same time—regardless of who is the witness and who the perpetrator of the action. According to one of the Italian neuroscientists who first identified these brain cells, Giacomo Rizzolatti, mirror neurons help explain how and why we "read" other people's minds and feel empathy for them. His United States colleague, Mark Iacoboni, added, "Mirror neurons tell us we're literally in the minds of other people." With our mirror neuron circuits firing simultaneously, we not only read and understand the other's intentions, we literally feel them in our own body.

The more I learned about mirror neurons, the more I came to think of my co-pilot beyond the Milky Way as "my mirror soul," my twin soul: the two of us forever connected no matter what, our brains lighting up with identical neural networks—parallel neurons in the very same areas of our brains firing simultaneously.* As in Iacoboni's description, the two of us could read,

---

*I was describing this "Forthward" to a dear friend who speaks fluent Spanish. She commented that the term "Mirror Soul" evoked for her the Spanish word *mirasol*, pronounced "me-rah-*sohl*." In Spanish, this word is the name for the sunflower, which always turns its face toward the light of the sun. Alternatively, she noted the other way to hear it is as two separate words, *mira sol*. Used this way, *mira sol* means "he (or she) sees the sun." As the word mirror suggests, my mirror soul is both source and reflector of light, a guiding star...

understand and feel the other, aware of the mirror's presence no matter where we were in time, place or space. This concept of mirror neurons and the mirror neural networks they form, sometimes called the "resonance circuitry" of the brain, helped explain the virtually ridiculous levels of synchronicity and resonance he and I shared between so many domains of our beings and our lives. Since our first joint carpet ride, it seemed that my mirror soul and I each inhabited the other, our mirror brain cells activated in sync, no matter where or with whom we were on the planet, no matter how strongly we fought it—no matter where we were in or out of time. Sometimes he would say in affirmation of the mirror: "Your experience is my experience. Everything you feel, I feel. Your reflections are my reflections."

And so, when my mirror soul died suddenly, unexpectedly, just days after I delivered the *Magic Carpet Flying* address to the graduates, my carpet was plunged into the deepest darkest abyss I had ever known. Not even my own words about light in the darkness—delivered what seemed to be a lifetime ago—could provide solace in this black, opaque vacuum into which my carpet had descended.

How does one detect light when all that can be seen is dark?

In those first agonizing days and nights following the death of my mirror soul, I did not know who I was. I didn't care. It took every ounce of strength I could muster just to place one foot in front of the other to walk, let alone eat. During the days, my body and brain surprisingly continued to function, as if on automatic or cruise control, ensuring that I at least appeared to those who did not know me, a normal, functioning human being. But the grief was so, so powerful. As I had noted in *Magic*

Carpet Flying, death, dying, loss and grief are familiar passengers on my carpet. Because I had travelled similar paths before, some part of me knew I would weather this battering storm. But who would I be in the aftermath? The grief now was like none I had ever known.

Just as our connection had not been on an earthly plane, it was fitting that the context for grieving would not be normal daily life. When I heard the devastating news, I was in Johannesburg, in transit to Uganda to do reconnaissance for some psychosocial work in war-affected communities. My mirror soul and I had had many potent conversations about Uganda. He had travelled there in the past and I had helped him prepare. I was now visiting some of the same places and peoples that had so impacted him. His experiences there had helped me prepare. I knew he would not want his death to prevent me from doing what I had set out to do. So I continued my travels, committed to

Uganda...a decision I will always treasure. During this surreal journey, the darkness surrounding my carpet was slowly infiltrated by small shafts of light, shafts that ultimately expanded to illuminate, once again, not only my carpet, but my flight path and the airspace in which I continue to fly.

The physical journey throughout Uganda involved traveling from the capital, Entebbe, to a town in the central north, called Lira. During our days in Lira, we drove out into the red African bush, visiting with people in various villages north of the town, which had so recently been a war zone. In these areas, many locals were slowly returning to their land after eight years in the nearby refugee camps. We visited villages that were being rebuilt after decimation by war and neglect. The land in some areas was so overgrown that previous landmarks made identification of property boundaries virtually impossible. This resulted in conflict among landowners. The locals, who had once deployed oxen and plows to work their fields, now did so by hand. In many villages, ancient social structures had been rendered obsolete by years of living in refugee camps. Extended families, if not torn apart by the death of family members, returned to villages only to find the youth deserting rural life for the towns and cities, often grouping together in gangs. Some of the gangs turned to crime to survive.

Although I felt like I was floating in a dream through these villages, the long Ugandan days were filled with unforgettable life-giving odysseys of the spirit. I was blessed to experience many touching meetings with local Ugandans— veterans of grief, who breathed light into their own histories, histories peppered with untold brutality and darkness. I bore witness to their stories of horror, and also their stories of rebirth that followed. These were people who accepted the trajectory of their carpet rides with grace and equanimity. Now, with faith in the tenuous peace agreement between the Ugandan government and the rebels' Lord's Resistance Army, they smiled and sang with hope as they tentatively allowed their carpets to rise again. Their focus on the future was clear testament to human triumph over years of volatility, war, poverty, loss, unimaginable hardship. In communion with these beautiful people, and in affinity with their stories, my own pain seemed to meld with the collective pain of all humanity.

How does one learn to be with the dark?

The nights in Uganda were filled with very different journeys…as I traversed the internal landscape of my own spirit. My carpet plummeted mentally, emotionally and physically—

registering the shock of my mirror soul's death, succumbing to the seemingly imponderable depths of sadness. It was as though I had sunk to the furthest depths of a bottomless chasm. All sounds and sights were muted by dark and immeasurable sorrow. It felt like I was at the very bottom of an infinitely deep well, all sounds and sights from the surface sensed only as a ripple in the silent depths far below. But the silence was screaming, screaming with a myriad of memories that rendered the present meaningless, lifeless.

Shafts of healing light slowly pierced the aching black void of those nights. The shafts materialized in the text messages and voices of loved ones from around the world, thanks to the miracle of global technology. My cherished "sisterhood" and family, rather than try to tell me I would be okay, metaphorically flew with me in the dark void, holding me, listening to me, talking me through the darkness, all the while respecting my knowledge that to embrace the dark and the pain was not a choice, but an imperative. Their voices were the tenuous bridge between the light and the dark. They coaxed me through those long hours, reminding me how much they loved me, how much they were there for me, what a gift my mirror soul was to me, and I to him. Just as they had basked in my glow during the height of my joy with my mirror soul, now they bolstered my entire being as I was catapulted through the abyss. They affirmed it was okay, too, to be angry with him. Okay to be angry that for so long he stubbornly adhered to the dominant script that ruled his life, angry that he would not or could not integrate into that dominant script the dogged, belligerent story his body and soul were so clearly trying to impress upon him. Okay to be angry that a vast multitude of potential unlived lives together was never to be, for both of us.

So my maelstrom of black thoughts was slowly infiltrated by pockets of color and light. My mind constantly performed mental pirouettes—one minute, smiling, when the tiniest of triggers transported me to the galaxies he and I visited together; the next minute, seized by sorrow that those galaxies were now part of the abyss.

How does one expand the light?

The palpable presence of my mirror soul was with me in every breath. I remembered how much light we gave to each other. I revelled in recollections of the delight, the joy and the love as my senses replayed our soaring through the cosmos, the meteor collisions and the venturing to unexplored celestial destinations, which, as he said, were "somewhere close to heaven." I recalled his voice noting that we had enriched each other's lives in more ways than we could imagine. In the wake of his death, I felt so thankful our mirrors had refracted so much light and richness to the other. I re-read the poetry we had read together, the words of T.S. Eliot, Mattie Stepanek, Kahlil Gibran, Lord Byron—all now imbued with the added potency of loss, of unrealized potential. And he was there, too, in the music I played on my iPod, music we had relished together, from the pulsating beat of our beloved Rolling Stones, to the mellifluous, transporting sounds of Andrea Bocelli.

So my journey to Uganda became a pilgrimage of sorts—a pilgrimage of my mind, my heart and my spirit.

After our travels through the villages around Lira, our group flew to the far northwest of the country. We headed to the larger town of Arua, in the corner of Uganda where three of the world's troubled countries converge: eight miles to the west is the Democratic Republic of the Congo; twenty miles to the north is Sudan. Arua is a bustling, diverse community that serves many of the surrounding districts, commercially, medically, politically. In the recent past, it has been a magnet for refugees from the Sudan and the Congo who fled the violence and horror of years of conflict in their own countries.

For our journey from Lira to Arua (some 300 miles), we flew in a small plane, a Cessna Caravan. Several months prior to this trip, I had made arrangements for me to fly these interior Ugandan journeys as the co-pilot. The day of the flight, I donned the co-pilot headset, scooted my seat up to the foot pedals and the yoke, eager to fly! My mirror soul was always particularly with me when I flew. A pilot himself, he was keenly interested in my flying adventures, quizzing me about every flight, relishing my descriptions of specific escapades, questioning me further about the minutia of each flying experience, sharing his own experiences and wisdom, particularly when he knew it would help if I felt less than confident about any maneuvers. He had been especially reassuring as I prepared for my first solo—humorously recalling his knocking knees during his first momentous flight alone to assuage my nervousness about my own. Given the constraints on his own opportunities to fly, he had told me—only weeks before—that he flew through me.

So as I took controls of the Cessna, citing "my airplane" as the signal that I was now piloting the plane, I was flying for both of us. My mirror soul was with me—and I was comforted by the knowledge that no matter where he was in the universe, both our mirror neural networks were firing with the exhilaration and elation that flying inevitably instilled in us, no matter what our moods.

We floated high above the magnificent,

dense, lush forests that appeared to spread from one side of Uganda to the other. Our flight path took us to 10,500 feet above sea level. Before long, we were soaring above the Nile, not far from where the Nile hurtles into Lake Albert, the vast body of water that blankets central Uganda. The vista was breathtaking. We could see the Nile meandering off into the distance, melding with the barely visible horizon. And as we flew, I was thinking to my mirror soul how much he, too, would be intoxicated by the stunning views and the exalting experience. Silently I told him how connected I felt to all of the peoples who lived along the Nile—from where our Cessna hovered above the endless landscape, all the way up to Egypt and the Middle East—peoples of so many different cultures and traditions. I voiced to him as well, the connection I equally felt with the entire history and future of humankind, embodied in the timeless flow of this powerful expanse of water:

a surging river of all humanity—past, present and future. I reiterated my timeless connection to him. I savored every second.

After crossing the Nile, we encountered a mammoth mass of clouds, voluminous vertically, horizontally and laterally—beautiful fluffy puffs of white in all directions. Because I was not yet certified to fly through clouds, I navigated the plane through all the spaces between the clouds, pockets of clear blue amid t puffs of white. I was immersed in the sheer joy of the flight—never more free...flying with him...dipping, diving, swerving right, then swerving left—instinctively and gleefully dancing through those pockets of blue, banki the plane one way, then the other, pitching down one minute, spiraling skyward the next. It was amazing. And the whole time I was thinking to my mirror soul. I silently recited to him the words of John MacGee's "High Flight":

Oh! I have slipped the surly bonds of Earth
And danced the skies on laughter-silvered
*   wings;*
Sunward I've climbed, and joined the tum-
*   bling mirth*
of sun-split clouds—and done a hundred
*   things....*

I've chased the shouting wind along, and flung
My eager craft through footless halls of air.
Up, up the long delirious, burning blue,
I've topped the windswept heights with easy
*   grace*
Where never lark, nor even eagle flew—
And, while with silent lifting mind I've trod
The high untresspassed sanctity of space....

When our two carpets first collided, my mirror soul described the physical sensation of his
heart literally swelling with the experience. In
those soaring moments in the vast skies above

the magnificent Ugandan landscape, I could feel my heart swelling with the rapture of all the magical past moments with him fused together in that palpable present.

After emerging from this floating in and out of time, I saw an opening between some clouds. The opening seemed to herald an expanse of clear blue sky beyond. This "gateway" was about a thousand feet higher than where we were flying, so I pitched up the plane and ascended toward the small portal through the mass of white. Up, up, up ... When we burst through, a spectacular panorama awaited us. Directly ahead was a stunning rainbow that stretched the entire width of the immediate horizon, a rainbow that appeared to be suspended down to earth from "somewhere close to heaven." My breath was taken away. I gasped. My swelling heart literally stopped. I thought it would explode. As I placed one hand on my chest (keeping the other on the yoke of the plane!), tears gently streamed down my face. I was engulfed by light in all its glory—literally every color of the rainbow. I could not only feel the glow of his light, but I could feel the glow that was surely emanating from the very cortex of my own brain. And I could not help but recall the poignant words of one of our favorite Rolling Stones songs my mirror soul and I had enjoyed together: "...I'll be the rainbow when this song is gone, wrap you in my color and keep you warm...." (from "That's How Strong My Love Is")

I looked to the rear of the plane where my dear friend and colleague was sitting. Tears flowed silently down her cheeks. As the angel who bore me the shattering news just days before, she, too, now felt wrapped in his color. We looked at each other in complete wonder at what we had just witnessed. And even more wondrous, playing on my friend's iPod at the very moment when we burst through the clouds was Josh Groban singing "To Where You Are":

Who can say for certain
Maybe you're still here
I feel you all around me
Your memories so clear

Deep within the stillness
I can hear you speak
You are still my inspiration....

And you are watching over me from up above?

Fly me up to where you are
Beyond the distant star
I wish upon tonight
To see you smile
If only for awhile to know you're there
A breath away's not far
To where you are....

This hauntingly magnificent rainbow turned
out to be just the first in a series of inconceiv-

able "encounters" with my mirror soul in the months following his death—encounters the scientist in me struggled to explain. After the second experience, the scientist surrendered. I no longer needed to explain. It was clear my mirror soul was still flying with me, lighting my way home—reminding me at key points along the way that he was there. My mirror soul was especially tenacious when my carpet faltered, not letting me forget that regardless of how black the darkness, there is always, always light. And haven't other scientists observed that even during a total eclipse of the sun, there is still light? During those rare daylight nights on earth, not only are the brightest stars in the universe revealed, but beads of sunlight are refracted through the moon's valleys, flaring out spectacular sprays of color from behind the dark disc. In that moment, soaring high above Uganda, I too was sprayed with color.

And now, as I write the final touches to this

Forthward, I look up to the view beyond my computer screen, out the window across the ocean. There in front of me spanning the blue horizon, is a rainbow peeping in and out of the low hanging clouds … I smile knowingly. How else could it be? Where else would my mirror soul be?

How does one sustain the light?

As I fly on, although still engulfed at unpredictable times by waves of sadness, I am not bereft. I carry his light inside me. I carry the light of my beloved friends and family. And I carry the light of my own life—with all of the peaks and all of the valleys. I carry, too, the knowledge that my carpet, despite having been routed through the blackest, starkest darkness—a darkness I could never have imagined—will continue to soar. As my mirror soul so exemplified in his own life's work, in the light that emanated so strongly from his smiling face, his entire being, these inevitable plunges are not only a life-giving part of any carpet ride, when examined with a different lens, they are the very source of light. And after all, wasn't this particular darkness, this seemingly bottomless black ravine, a reflection of the summit of the love so intensely felt between twin souls, mirror souls? And wasn't that love about enlightenment, about exploring new ways of seeing and being, about being lit up?

And maybe that's the point. This carpet ride can be magic if life is experienced fully, lived intensely—in all its wondrous colors—from the darkest black to the lightest white, and every possible hue of the rainbow in between.

Credits

As with humankind's first attempts to become airborne off the sand dunes of Kitty Hawk in North Carolina over 100 years ago, flying a carpet magically is not characterised by smooth, effortless, efficient flight. The first human forays into the skies were literal "hops" ranging from just 35 to 262 metres. Journeys into outer space just sixty years later, mere flights of the imagination in 1903! When a book takes flight, the writing also comes in fits and spurts, and it is not until way into the journey that the semblance of a flight-path is discernible. And a successful flight and safe landing are only assured with the encouragement, nurturing, support, and cheering not immediately obvious if we only focus on the cockpit.

It was never my intent that these reflections be published into a book, let alone my first. So many other books have long been competing in my head to be released onto typed pages! But in the spirit of zig-zagging, I embraced the flow of the universe and the gentle nudging of publisher, Patrick Boyer! It was Patrick's vision, enthusiasm, patience and faith that gave this book wings. And it was Patrick's team at Blue Butterfly Books, especially Dominic Farrell and Gary Long, who made sure the pages were ready to fly—despite the obstacles created by its strong-willed author!

This particular flight of words has benefitted from the support and encouragement of so many people. I will always be indebted to the indefatigable IDA team, the dream team of public policy think tanks. In particular, Toula Skiadas, Anna Burchett, and Sarah Cotton, as always, provided scrutinising editing and helpful comments before these words approached the runway.

The Forthward especially would not exist without the sheer brilliance, wit, compassion, and staying power of my "sisterhood." Isadora James said that a sister is "a gift to the heart, a friend to the spirit, a golden thread to the meaning of life." I am blessed with such a sisterhood—family and friends of all ages and walks of life (including some very special men!)—who shelter and strengthen me, no matter what turbulence surrounds me. My "sisters" embraced the Forthward as the healing salve it was...not just for me, but for others as well. Thank you to Virginia Hickey, Susanne Cole and Jane Knowler in particular, for their wise counsel on various renditions of these words, as well as in life. This writing process was also especially enriched by Kelly Young and Karen Skelton, whose incisive comments are always tempered with love and good ol' Texan fun. Moira Deslandes, my "sister" for over thirty years, who is there no matter what, read virtually every draft of the Forthward, and never failed to suggest ways to make it better. As with all my sisters and brothers, her presence in the universe makes my life better.

And to my immediate family, who daily grace my magic carpet, how lucky am I? You bear with me when I lavish so much time on flying—both literal and metaphorical, lift me up when I am down, and shower me with magic every day.

Finally, one of the many blessings since my Mirror Soul died has been the evolving sisterhood with his mum, who opened her heart, shared her precious memories, and relished listening to mine. Not long before he died, my Mirror Soul, who had once lamented that he wished he had my sisterhood to help him through a particular period of turmoil, was bestowed honorary membership in that sisterhood. His smile and his voice live on in both my heart and my head. My writing (and my flying!) is enhanced because he is there.

About the Author

Born in Australia and now holding dual citizenship as an American and Australian, Pamela Ryan is driven by the conviction that all humans are born equal in capacity but not opportunity. This belief has fueled her lifelong endeavor to help bring voice to the voiceless, whether in the business, social, or political arenas.

For thirty years, Ryan has been committed to facilitating equality and social justice through her direct involvement as a psychologist, an educator (on university campuses in both Australia and the United States), through political activity, and in public policy advocacy.

A firm believer in the potential benefits of "scrambling" one's structured view of the world, Pamela delights to shine light on new ways of doing things—whether for individuals, groups, organizations, communities, or nations. She regularly scrambles her own life, having reincarnated herself as a psychologist in several distinct arenas—corporate, political, clinical, academic, and international humanitarian. All of these "lives" came together in her work with Psychology Beyond Borders, which she co-founded in 2006.

Passionate about education being a fundamental right of all citizens, and the very foundation of democracy, Ryan's role as managing director of Issues Deliberation Australia/America has involved numerous leading-edge national and international public policy and research initiatives, such as building understanding between Muslims and non-Muslims, reconciliation between indigenous and non-indigenous Australians, feasibility of human rights legislation and parliamentary reform, "future perfect thinking" about economic development, comparisons of voters' mental maps, and exploration of psychological well-being in the face of fear and terror.

Pamela is also committed to ensuring those born into environments with less opportunity and resources get a better deal. In 2000 she co-founded and continues to chair the board of the Texas-based Silverton Foundation, which focuses on empowerment of disadvantaged peoples in the United States, Australia, and other parts of the world such as Ethiopia, East Timor, Sri Lanka, India, Vietnam, and South Africa.

Author or co-author of many public policy reports, conference papers, and academic articles relating to Issues Deliberation subjects and Psychology Beyond Borders projects, Dr. Ryan has also given countless public presentations.

When not immersed in the work that so inspires and sustains her, Pamela succumbs to her "inner sports fanatic." Ingrained during her upbringing in the Australian outback, she revels in any outdoor activity, being an avid swimmer, cyclist, and flier of single-engine planes. She also maintains her balance by regularly practicing Kundalini yoga and pilates, hiking with her Irish setters, and hanging out with family and friends over robust conversation, food, and wine.

This photo was taken on the day I heard my Mirror Soul had died. I did not know this photo existed until about nine months later … and I shed a tear when I saw it as my mind revisited the darkness of that day. I was in South Africa at that time, at Boikarebelo, a village of some 150 kids who have been orphaned by AIDS and other tragedies. I had not told anyone about my Mirror Soul dying, but was clearly not myself (this was not my first visit to the village). In the midst of conversation with the wonderful founders of Boikarebelo, Con and Marion Cloete, one of the young boys climbed onto a chair, spontaneously spread out his arms, and said "hug." Marion smiled and said, "He knows who needs love today." This moment was particularly moving to me, because this gorgeous little boy, who had been born into such darkness (he was found at age six months in a box, freezing cold and severely malnourished), was able to so unexpectedly reach out to me in my darkness and embrace me with light ….

Interview with the Author

When you first addressed your "magic carpet flying" message to university graduates, I understand the convocation ceremonies became emotional. What happened?

PAMELA RYAN: I talked about personal subjects few people dare to visit out loud—mental illness, suicide, the dark side of the human condition. Friends and colleagues said the 2,500 people in the audience were riveted. I could see many quietly crying about my experiences in some of life's darkest moments, but I also heard them laughing loudly when I talked about some humorously embarrassing moments! All that, of course, is in this book.

Anything else?

RYAN: Many graduates crossing the stage after receiving their degrees turned to say "thank you!" One even threw his degree certificate to the floor in front of me with a sweeping flourish, knelt on both knees so close his eyes were a foot away from mine, and said, "Thank you *sooo* much."

Apparently these kinds of reactions had not been witnessed at a graduation ceremony before. So clearly, the experiences I related from my life resonated with them. These reactions were very moving for me, too, because this was the first time anyone in our family had publicly discussed what we had endured.

Few writers put pen to paper without hoping someone out there will read their words. Who do you see as your audience for Magic Carpet Flying?

RYAN: *Magic Carpet Flying* was initially written for graduates in psychology, social work, anthropology, and communications at the University of South Australia, as well as the families, friends, and faculty with whom they would be celebrating their achievement and this rite of passage. This was a different writing experience for me, because most of my writing typically addresses academic or public policy subjects.

I also knew my daughters would probably one day read it so I wanted *Magic Carpet Flying* to carry messages that could resonate with them as well. They were thus part of the "audience."

Also, I wrote for myself, to discover whether what I had learned in fifty years of living was worth sharing. I love how ideas evolve when we try to form them into coherent written expressions, but it is rare that we play with ideas touching the deepest issues of our lives.

So in terms of audience, I saw the opportunity to craft a message for young graduates as a way of reaching the graduates, my daughters, and anyone else who had faced the harrowing darkness of mental illness in their own lives.

Then with your invitation to publish *Magic Carpet Flying* as a Blue Butterfly book, I hoped the audience might be extended to other people curious about how the flight metaphor could help them frame this journey we call life and navigate the inevitable ascents and descents through both light and dark.

But in this book you've added to that original message, haven't you?

RYAN: Yes. When someone I called "my mirror soul" died, shortly after I delivered my address, I wrote for myself in the form of writing to him. He loved my writings to him, and would read and re-read my letters. So strange as it sounds, the so-called "Forthward," which is now included in this book as you note, was actually to myself and to him.

It is intensely private and personal writing.

RYAN: I have always found writing to be particularly healing, and research proves I am not alone in this experience. Expressive writing for several consecutive days can have dramatic positive physical, mental, and emotional impacts.

Once I had said everything I wanted to say in the Forthward, I decided to share it with my closest friends so they might understand not just my journey into the black abyss, but the beautiful, life-giving role they themselves had played in my journey back out of the darkness. Upon reading it, some cautiously encouraged me to include this piece as part of my *Magic Carpet Flying* book.

After great soul-searching and consideration of potential consequences for me and others, I accepted that the Forthward was actually integral to my own mental map of *Magic Carpet Flying* because my "mirror soul" had been such an indelible aspect of my carpet ride. He was with me in every word of that address to the graduates. Given his death within days of my delivering it, to not include this story, which is quintessential to who I am today, would have meant not living my own truth.

Well, that uniquely named Forthward is part of this book now, thanks to your candour.

RYAN: Inclusion of the Forthward broadens the audience to those who find themselves feeling irrevocably deluged by darkness, and those who have been irrevocably engulfed by light! In shar-

ing this excruciatingly personal journey, I hope
that in reading one person's odyssey toward
light, readers discover in their own darkness, as
John O'Donahue so hauntingly described in
Beannacht, "a path of yellow moonlight to bring
them safely home."

*What do you hope someone reading this
book might discover?*

RYAN: Other than "a path of yellow moonlight?" That life always contains both darkness
and light. That we can get through the darkness,
no matter how horrendous. That we can revel in
the light, even if the illumination is only fleeting.

*Your openness about private life is refresh-
ing in an age of manipulated messages, so what
is needed in the way of courage to share intimate
thoughts and emotions with strangers?*

RYAN: I did not view the candour about my
own life as courage-based. It was more like an
imperative to talk about these things, particularly my dad's schizophrenia and suicide.

I have always valued truth and honesty, and in the last ten years or so of my life particularly, I have striven toward living my "truth." I know that sounds clichéd but throughout the first half of my life, always percolating in the background, was the massive secret about Dad. In those days, and even now to some degree, a diagnosis of mental illness is accompanied by tremendous stigma. The negative and often uninformed reactions of others to a diagnosis of schizophrenia or any mental illness can be very hurtful and feed the distress, even the illness itself.

At the time my father killed himself, neither mental illness nor suicide was publicly or openly discussed. So my mother, acting out of protection for us and my father, fought to ensure Dad's suicide was kept a secret, even to keep that label from his death certificate.

As a result, although we discussed the circumstances of his death within our family, to anyone else, we would say his death was the outcome of a shooting accident. That worked for us at the time. I have no doubt that the "secret" protected us from the further emotional distress of public discussion of suicide at a time when it was such a taboo topic.

But while I appreciated our mother's protec-

tive instincts, as an adult I railed against the
conspiracy of silence. In the silence was still
a lie. It was a lie I found myself perpetuating
with my own children—"until they were old
enough to handle the truth." And that was a
dilemma. I understand there are developmen-
tally appropriate ages at which to reveal certain
truths to children, yet I am also aware from my
work as a psychologist that when we maintain
a conspiracy of silence about mental illness and
suicide we unwittingly perpetuate stigma, injustice, and distress to those who suffer as well as
to the loved ones who suffer along with them.
Research shows that while we may attempt to
maintain the silence by not talking about the
secret with words, other conveyors of knowledge
unconsciously transmit the messages anyway.

This means we can perpetrate hurt on future
generations by not being open and truthful
about the reality of what happened, prolonging
the conspiracy. It is no coincidence that suicide
rates are higher in families where there has been
suicide. We cannot change those statistics nor
the tragic human stories behind them unless
we talk graciously, candidly, and informatively
about these painful afflictions.

So is that openness a requirement of "freedom," then?

RYAN: Freedom for me is being able to speak and live truth with grace, respect, dignity, and without fearing the ramifications. Freedom is being able to be who I am. Freedom is the opportunity and capacity to forge through all the frontiers—emotional, physical, social, spiritual, and intellectual.

And as a magic carpet flier?

RYAN: Freedom is soaring above the landscape without ever losing sight of the gifts the land below also offers. Freedom is knowing, when the carpet I ride plummets into darkness, that I have soared before and can soar again, just as never forgetting when I am soaring through light, what it feels like to be in darkness.

As an airplane pilot you must get, not in imagination but reality, a detached overview of the landscape. How does this influence your own take on life?

RYAN: Flying a plane I simultaneously experience exhilaration and trepidation, depending on just how confident I am in my skill level on any given day and the conditions in which I am flying. The same is true in daily life, as well. That is why the flight metaphor can enrich our understanding of life's journey. To fly above the minutia of daily life gives a distanced perspective otherwise difficult to attain, an ability to see the big picture.

Yet hovering above the landscape is not a detached perspective, as you suggest. The skyscape is really part of the landscape. As a pilot, I must be aware of both the sky and the land, constantly assessing the conditions, adjusting my flying to suit what I am experiencing every moment, all the while aware of moving toward my desired destination.

So it's a question of balance?
RYAN: Exactly. Sometimes we get so immersed in the routines and the doing that we forget to notice what we are feeling in the moment, for-

get that we are actually soaring high above the earth. By the same token, we sometimes get so absorbed in soaring that we fail to remember what's on the ground. So I must always strive to remain aware when I am flying that what I am experiencing in any given moment—the thrill, or the panic—could change in an instant.

My favorite time to fly is at night: with the glistening lights of a sprawling city below, and the infinite expanse of stars in the blackness all around me. I am particularly reminded in those moments how exhilarating it is to fly. Both the lights on the ground and the stars in the sky provide the joy. And I relish every opportunity I have to soar, whether on the ground or in the stratosphere beyond the Milky Way, because who knows when I might plummet again!

You offer leadership in women's health, and in the well-being of those who survive terrorist attacks and natural disasters. In Australia you work for the reconciliation of cultural differences between Aborigines and non-Aborigines, Muslims and non-Muslims, monarchists and republicans. What "spark from heaven," as Shakespeare would put it, did you "pick up" that causes you to do this?

RYAN: I am glad you quote Shakespeare! Although a devotee, I could not weave his work into *Magic Carpet Flying* so I am happy you have!

I am not sure the source of the "spark," but yes, I feel a compulsion to do what I do. Sometimes that spark is a veritable electric storm!

I grew up in a mining town of hard-working parents. Both were incredibly smart and talented, but limited by their life circumstances. For them, extended education was out of the question, just as it was for many with whom I went through primary and secondary school. My parents were "working class," but nothing about them was typical: my father learned to fly a plane in his late teens, and other than being a pilot, my mother could do anything my father could, including working alongside him building our family home. And regardless of their own income, they were silently, unassumingly, exceedingly compassionate and philanthropic. My mother instilled the message we were no better nor worse than any other human on the planet. She said that no matter how much or little we had, it was our responsibility to share with those who might be down on their luck. Our backyard was full of apricot, apple, orange, lemon, mandarin, and almond trees, as well as grape and passion fruit vines. When ripe, we picked the fruit and walked around our modest neighbourhood with buckets of fruit to deliver to anyone who wanted it, but particularly those who needed it. My dad did "humanitarian" air-drops for people stranded by flood or drought in the outback, and occasionally flew the Flying Doctor to surrounding districts.

So this "spark"—this drive for egalitarianism and social justice, my sense of responsibility to do something when I see injustice, but in a way that respects others' dignity—was instilled in me from a very early age.

Your work focuses on empowering disadvantaged peoples in the United States, Australia, Ethiopia, East Timor, Sri Lanka, India, Vietnam, and South Africa. You have elsewhere described this as helping people "see the light in the darkness." Is it really just a matter of inspiration, or are practical steps also needed for such empowerment, too?

RYAN: It is true that in my international work "empowerment" is a key theme. I am a huge believer in the innate resiliencies and natural light that people have within them, and some may not even realize they have. So these initiatives are geared to help people build on their own strength and to expand their light. But yes, this is often done through practical steps too, like providing information, education, and collaboration.

Sometimes empowerment can be physical. For example, in the decimated beach areas of Sri Lanka after the tsunami, a group of mothers was attempting to rebuild their lives and community, to re-establish livelihoods out of seaweed-strewn rubble. When asked what would help the most, one woman used her hands to make circles around her eyes. The problem was that some of the older women who'd swum for their lives to flee the gigantic wave had lost their eyeglasses. Once we provided replacements, they were again able to safely cook meals, help their kids with homework, and earn a living. So providing glasses was one such practical step.

In other situations, the practical steps are micro-financing a small home business, a family literacy program so everyone can learn together, or teaching basic psychosocial skills to health-care workers so they can respond more effectively to those they are trying to help emerge from their darkness.

Why did you create the international organization "Psychology Beyond Borders?"

RYAN: It was an organization waiting to happen! As a psychologist, I became quite disturbed after the attacks of September 11, 2001, by the level of fear being fuelled across America, even in communities far from areas at risk of future attacks. The fear seemed to be fuelled by political, community, and media leaders. When I asked several prominent politicians what they would do not to scare people, I was met with vague answers.

At that time, very few people were discussing or researching the psychology of terror and how to manage it. So in 2004 I brought together a group of the world's experts on fear and terror, and for three days in Texas we shared learning from various parts of the globe, from multiple disciplines, about how to manage the psychology of fear and terror.

What happened?

RYAN: One recommendation was to establish an organization that could dispatch multidisciplinary rapid response teams in the aftermath of a catastrophic event to assist communities manage the psychological and social havoc wreaked by mass tragedy, especially where local resources are limited.

It soon became clear that our mission was evolving far beyond psychosocial service delivery in the wake of an initial crisis. We discovered the need for an organization committed to combining research with service delivery in order to contribute to the body of knowledge about what most eases distress in circumstances of mass tragedy, and to use such knowledge to improve preparedness and response. For example, one thing learned from September 11 was that despite best intentions and sincere belief in the healing potential of particular therapeutic approaches, some practices actually can add to long-term distress rather than alleviate it.

So as Psychology Beyond Borders evolved, the more we saw the need to research the impact of psychosocial services practiced all over the planet. With better knowledge about what works best in which circumstances and for which people, we can now disseminate that knowledge so that survivors experience healing, rather than harmful, practices.

It seems like you are not just an airplane pilot and a magic carpet flyer, but even a blue butterfly!

RYAN: [Answers only with a beaming smile.]

Irish-born performing artist Treasa O'Driscoll was enjoying international success when her husband, a noted Celtic studies scholar, began a long descent into mental illness. Her story of her voyage through life is filled with joy, tragedy, and inspiration.

Celtic Woman: A Memoir of Life's Poetic Journey
Treasa O'Driscoll
ISBN 978-0-9781600-2-9
$24.95 USA/Canada

In this selection from her many insightful newspaper columns, journalist, teacher, mother, and community volunteer Patricia Boyer offers messages of wisdom and inspiration based on her observations of everyday events unfolding around her.

The March of Days: Optimistic Realism through the Seasons of Life
Patricia M. Boyer
ISBN 978-0-9784982-1-4
$22.95 USA/Canada

Author's royalties from the sale of
Magic Carpet Flying are being donated to
Psychology Beyond Borders.

For more information on this organization, visit

www.psychologybeyondborders.org

or contact

Psychology Beyond Borders
1000 Rio Grande, Austin, Texas, 78701 USA
Tel. 1-512-579-3825   Fax 1-512-579-3826